EAST OF MYLOONA

BY

ANDREW SUKNASKI

EAST OF MYLOONA © Copyright 1979 by Andrew Suknaski

ISBN   0-920066-21-6 (paper)
ISBN   0-920066-22-4 (cloth)

Book design by Neil Wagner.
Drawings by Andrew Suknaski. Any reproductions of the drawings of this book without the expressed permission of the publisher and/or the author/artist are prohibited.

Published Fall 1979 by

Thistledown Press
668 East Place
Saskatoon, Sask.
S7J 2Z5

CANADIAN CATALOGING IN PUBLICATION DATA

Suknaski, Andrew, 1942 -
East of Myloona

Poems.
Includes Index.
ISBN   0-920066-22-4 bd.
ISBN   0-920066-21-6 pa.

I. Title.
PS8587.U45E2   C811'.5'4   C79-091194-9
PR9199.3.S84E2

ACKNOWLEDGEMENTS

Hunter Stranded on an Ice Floe first appeared in WHALE SOUND, an anthology edited by Greg Gatenby and published by J.J. Douglas of Vancouver.

The drawing of Tom Doornbos first appeared as a cover for PERIODICS, a magazine of prose published in Vancouver.

"Young Inuit Art Student" first appeared in CANADIAN POETRY MAGAZINE.

The excerpt from Eddie Bazie's poem "For the Old People" was reprinted from NATIVE PRESS in Yellowknife.

The author is grateful for the editorial improvements of Glen Sorestad in the final restructuring of the manuscript. The author would also like to acknowledge the assistance of The Canada Council for providing the travel grant that helped make this book possible.

The publisher gratefully acknowledges the assistance of The Saskatchewan Arts Board and The Canada Council.

A couple of summers ago, suffering wilderness withdrawal (my first urban summer in 17 years) I grew bored writing prairie poems — clearly a Western Guilt Dream overload. So I bought a copy of NORTHERN FRONTIER, NORTHERN HOMELAND — Thomas R. Berger's report on the Mackenzie Valley Pipeline Inquiry. I read it twice. Fell in love with the voices: people speaking about the meaning of home, land, kinship, and so many aboriginal things. In time, the ache to travel that way grew too strong — I simply had to go, to better understand for myself something of what Judge Berger and Northerners were talking about. I hoped things would become clear, but they only became more confused.

What these poems grew from is a remembered NORTH. What people who became friends said, or might have said, or what I believe (in my vague and brief knowledge of a few Northern friends) they might possibly stand for. And I apologize to them if my imagination got carried away with actual facts and convictions. Anyway, for any failings of memory or imaginary tangents that may depart from the facts, I hope my Northern friends will forgive me. All I regret is that I did not go that way sooner.

Andrew Suknaski
Regina, March 1979

to MISHA and MAKITUK
of CAPE DORSET
wherever they are
now

*I was born in the Yukon, and that country
we always call it "Myloona"; that means
"where I hunted".*

ISHMAEL ALUNIK
President, The Hunters and
Trappers Association of Inuvik

*Our Dene nation is like this great river.
It has been flowing before any of us can remember.
We take our strength, our wisdom and our ways
from the flow and direction which has been
established for us by ancestors we never knew,
ancestors of a thousand years ago. Their wisdom
flows through us to our children and our grandchildren,
to generations we will never know. We will live
out our lives as we must, and we will die in peace
because we will know that our people and this river
will flow on after us.*

FRANK T'SELEIE
Fort Good Hope Band

TABLE OF CONTENTS

MAP / COMPASS

map? yous lookin at it!
compass? yous lookin at it!

wind from the NORTH
on yer back
in winter
white man
follow me!

1979

PACIFIC WESTERN FLIGHT NORTH

early morning light
and flying NORTH
                         surveyed northern farmlands fading
back
to become mauve horizon
of morning

        . . . it is true
        we had our chance once
        to do things right
        but botched it
        blinded by love for what
        we called   our country

        low lying mist
        serpentining along rivers

                             ATHABASCA

                    BIRCH

               PEACE

        SLAVE

        . . . there was
        another people
        with their own DREAM
        spanning these vast plains
        and parkland
        . . . touching earth
        they yearned for country
        and HOME
                 . . . denied
        by those who could not
        touch earth

A R R I V A L !

FORT SMITH

wind burnished faces
natives
and others
boarding for YELLOWKNIFE
NORMAN WELLS
INUVIK
and other destinations

                       aspen poplars turning
                                      yellow
                       a distinct feeling
                       of autumn
                       pervading the air
                                    still summer
                       back on the prairie

1977 / 1979

TJAR DOORNBOS

"You don't have a will, the will has you.
You come on this blink'n planet
when you are born with a message
and you fulfill that message
every split second."

TOM DOORNBOS

1

NORTH of no south
speak of LOVE
if you will

witness the small children
native and white
               innocently playing
               stop
               to honour old age
               with irrefutable love
               DOORNBOS of YELLOWKNIFE
               THE KING OF THE RAVENS*
               going uptown for his mail
               and daily coffee

listen to the children
call
with reverent affection

               "hello tom . . .

                              hi tom . . .

hello tom . . ."

               witness **THE KING OF THE RAVENS**
               whose egyptian blue eyes
               even the ravens
               stop to glimpse
                        ravenous ravens
               suddenly motionless
               in profound
                   silence

witness the small children
watching the tall stooped man amble
so slow
     slowly moving taller than myth
     THE KING OF THE RAVENS
     stately
     in the long winterspringsummerandfall
     black coat
          THE KING OF THE RAVENS
          knuckling a juniper cane
          walking
          slowly
          so slowly
          so slowly
          that all time seems to slide
          across the vast
          margins

NORTH of no south
dreaming of intangible answers
regarding HOPE
and HOME
abandoned
        listen to THE KING OF THE RAVENS scowl
        "Man . . . don't ask so many questions!"

witness the old man alone
revere each moment
transfigured by the warmth of lonely coffee
in the glow of the miners' mess
of the yellowknife inn
the old man wistfully watching
a girl and boy
holding hands
        . . . do they realize
        that these are the best years
        of their life?

2

soup in the miners' mess
a spoon suspended

DOORNBOS reflecting
                    "if you want something
                    try and get it
                    . . . if you fail
                    try again
                    an again
                    . . . then suddenly
                    it will come to you"

spoon dipping
into the blue enamel cup
                    "you don't realize
                    what a beautiful country you have
                    . . . the 30's
                    you should have seen your country
                    the first train i took
                    . . . hopped a freight
                    that was something
                    sitting on top of the boxcar
                    an seeing the country
                    jumped off in arcola
                    saskatchewan
                    no jobs
                    no place to go
                    so i come this way

                    . . . was born in 1891
                    province of gronin
                    northern holland
                    you know the romans
                    never conquered us
                    . . . europe
                    1914
                    everyone was happy
                    content
                    five years later
                    it was all haywire
                    . . . had a sweetheart
                    back in holland
                    i wanted to go to canada
                    lady loved me
                    but wouldn't come with me
                    this way
                    . . . you don't realize
                    what a beautiful country you have
                    if i could live my life over
                    i would leave that girl again
                    take the same train
                    an come this way
                    do some of the same things"

soup finished
DOORNBOS rising
to pull a xeroxed poem
from his pacific western
flightbag

                    "i'm still looking for my woman
                    . . . you got a girl?
                    give her this . . ."

spidery calligraphy reading

Tom's overcoat is thin
His hope is . . . on beyond.
Sally's shoes and gloves are worn
But see her diamond.

"remember . . .
if you want something
try and get it
. . . if you fail
try again
an again
. . . then suddenly
it will come to you"

DOORNBOS rising
to slowly lumber over
to a framed photograph
slowly hanging his cup there
from a hook

3

photograph/

DOORNBOS
wearing a 30's tweed cap

beneath the brim
a coal black shadow
reminiscent
of a quarter moon

eyes squinting

the face

mirroring glare

of the bright

NORTHERN SUN

DOORNBOS
lugging water
1942 to 1946
two pails at a time

grateful villagers and cafes
of old YELLOWKNIFE
paying two-bits a pail
for spring water

to the right of the photograph
and others

    a great wooden framework
    with hooks
    suspending a hundred enamel cups
    all numbered
    framework and cups
    from the original
    miners' mess
    at the mine

DOORNBOS
ceasing odd jobs
in the late 60's
due to
a weakening
heart

4

CARE
    the DREAM transmuting
    the playing children's cries
    in the dark
    of cold winter days
    in the NORTH

        HOPE
            the leathery sounds
            of snow
            under feet
            of the homebound
            man

LOVE
    the juniper cane
    leaning
    outside
    against the wall
    by the blue door reading
    number 7
    in the yellowknife
    old folks home

    "that way . . . they know
    at night
        i'm in

    and don't have to
    worry . . .
    about me"

1977 / 1979

* *Tom Doornbos holds 11% of the shares of one of Yellowknife's two gold mines. The raven is the city's official emblem. THE KING OF THE RAVENS comes from nobler lineage — and claims all his wealth will go to worthy causes and institutions in the North West Territories.*

ICON AND AXE

PHOTO
      and AXE

beyond the young
white girl
standing
      to pour sugar and cream
      into the cup
      of coffee
      before the blind
      INDIAN boy
            gazing beyond the edge
            of her glowing face

1977 / 1979

OLIVER POWDER

gold range pub
OLIVER POWDER enjoying
the first molson's canadian
in weeks

OLIVER POWDER
METIS trapper from TWIN LAKES
40 miles NORTH
of YELLOWKNIFE
                    OLIVER POWDER fondly speaking
                    of his SLAVEY wife
                    their two sons
                    and twin daughters

                    his father
                    and grandfather CHIEF JOSEPH
                    CREE

OLIVER POWDER
against urban lifelessness
                    diffusing from the south
against "that three nation idea
                    of the NORTH"
against government plans to survey
                    and redistribute divided land
                    for smaller traplines

"boy . . . i got guns
many guns boy!
my father trapped on the land
i now trap on
and he worked *hard*
hard boy
to feed us
. . . and i work hard
to feed my family
government wanna divide my land?
they'll have to come with *guns* boy! *guns!*
and they'll have to be able
to shoot *well*
cauz i got *guns* boy!
ain't nobody's gonna survey
across my traplines
. . . they try?
they're gonna have to set up that tripod
over my dead body
cauz i got *guns* boy!"

1977 / 1979

THE MINERS' MESS IN THE YELLOWKNIFE INN

along the walls
tables for two
         and in the middle
         several simple wooden tables
         for ten
                  on the south wall hang
                  black and white photographs
                  of miners

                  the plaque
                  above a rusty pick reads:

                  original negus mine
                  found by arctic divers
                  in 30 feet of water
                  just out from old
                  negus mine

left of the pick
two METIS girls whisper
over coke
words of possible love

above them
stand three white miners
in a photograph:

TOM HANSON
SAM OTTO
BILL JOHNSON

HARDING LAKE 1939

there are no imaginary boundaries
drawn here
           paying black tribute
           to some dead zone
           of the brain

           white or native
           you sit where you please

1977 / 1979

ALEX TAWYE

10 a.m. opening time
gold range pub in YELLOWKNIFE
ALEX TAWYE is the first
retired native trapper there
ALEX clad in red hudson bay jacket
savours a cool one
when i quietly ask
                "mind if i join you?"
then turns
"waiter . . . two more pil!"

ALEX's face
the colour of dark precambrian stone reveals
faintly discernible suspicion
while he inquires
eyeing my united grain growers cap
"weh you frum?"

                "down south
                southern saskatchewan"

"mhhhhh . . . flahtlonder
dhat be deh place queen veektoria
she giff dhem each
trahpline . . . one mile
one mile!
           how kin fahlah live on dhat?

maybe hunder fitty mile
                queen veektoria
                giff one mile
ha ha ha ha! one mile!
fahlah fahmily stahv to death . . . me um trahper"

i tug my cap brim lower
pry further
"tell me about your grandfather
was he a trapper too?"

                              "no . . . whok foh hutzah bay
pahddl kahnoe . . . cahrry stuff
sometime pohtage
yah knoh?
                    wok ah summih
                    foh muzzahlohdda
                    ah summih
                    jiss one muzzahlohdda . . ."

raised right hand
ALEX's thumb and index finger
encompassing his right glimmering eye

                    "ten lead ball
                    muzzahlohdda!
                    ten ball
                    dhat big!
                    foh ah summih
                    whok foh hutzah bay"

"my god! that's all?
for a whole summer?"

                    "hutzah bay
                    ho summih!"

"jesus . . . that's sad ALEX
men like your grandfather
working in those days
for next to nothing
to help build all those stores now
as big as cathedrals
down south . . . god!
that's sad . . .
sad . . ."

                    "dhot foh sure
                    yah . . . the hutzah bay
                    yah . . . sod
                    dhot foh sure!"

1977 / 1979

INUVIK

INUVIK
>"... PLACE OF MAN"

INUVIK
>Once the place JOHN ADAMS
>set his traps
>till it was surveyed
>in 1955

INUVIK
>once home for 4000
>half-native
>>INUIT
>>DENE
>>and METIS
>and half
>immigrants
>from southern canada

1977
late summer
population approximately
3200

>"the others?
>gone man ... gone!
>ain't no pipeline comin through!"
>the voice like lazarus
>returning from the dead

i continue down mackenzie road
past IGLOO
the roman catholic church
to walk along the board walkway

two INUIT men with canes
slowly shuffling past
one nodding

                    "good day sir"

                              i respond
                    in what seems
                    unusual light
                    of the late evening

a few paces further
native children by IGLOO
across the street
calling
                    "HI HIPPIE!"

i muble a faint "hi . . ."
move on
to continue where
stunted aspen poplars
have begun to turn colour
and on to tamarack forest
suddenly stopping
to see the wide MACKENZIE

. . . somewhere NORTH
still further
THE DELTA begins
. . . the place where the ashes
of a catholic priest
who served the people
of this place
have become earth
plant
and finned flesh . . .

beyond the
            mewling cries
of distant
            sea birds
that draw no boundaries
            between themselves

1977 / 1979

SHAMAN ANGATKROK

*carving in bowhead whale vertebra
and moose teeth, 1976*

SHAMAN ANGATKROK

       ANGATKROK

      "whale /
             . . . honouring the whale"

SHAMAN ANGATKROK

      carved by
ABRAHAM APAKARK ANGHIK
born 1951
of **ESKIMO**
nomadic family
home
PAULATUK
250 miles **NORTH**
of the arctic circle

listen . . .

      who does the bone
      transfigured ghost
      of SHAMAN ANGATKROK
      curse?

         the white prospector?
         white surveyors?
         the miners bringing southern diseases?
         white bootleggers?
         the highway builders?
         the grafting southern merchants?

      who knows?
      but let a single white ghost pass
      along betraying void of frontier

and SHAMAN ANGATKROK's
moose teeth
will draw blood!

1977 / 1979

INUKPAK

INUKPAK
    bigger than a cloud's
    shadow

moving across
            INUK
                    "ONE PERSON"

AGNES SEMMLER
OF INUVIK
        telling her favorite
        children's story
        THE DREADFUL TOWERING GIANT

            INUKPAK

        taller than a MOUNTAIN

        . . . INUKPAK come walkin
        and he juggle these BIG BOULDER
        he come walkin
        earth shake!
        and he blot out SUN
        INUKPAK
                shadow!

        It fall like NIGHT
        over this native village
        people
        they go to MEDICINE MAN
        say
            "SAVE US FROM INUKPAK!
            GO TALK TO HIM!"

MEDICINE MAN go
speak to STONE GIANT!
HE stop
       . . . listen
turn
      an walk out into SEA

there ISLAND there now
in CORONATION BAY
where COPPERMINE
flow to SEA
          there some HOLES . . .
        in EARTH there
they lead to place
where you see ISLAND
they say
      that ISLAND
       top of INUKPAK'S head
these marks in EARTH
      . . . HIS FOOTSTEPS!

1977 / 1979

HENRY RIVETT

RIVETT strumming *blue moon of kentucky*
while the MACKENZIE flows on

RIVETT
        ho-ho——ing
        humming through water

RIVETT
        nose and mouth dipping
        to rise from a bowl of water
        three days after presley's journey
        beyond the dark valley

        ". . . you see elvis
        wen he use to sing *blue moon* . . .
        he use to hit them
        LOOOoow notes!
        i could never hit them
        you know?
        so i tried this new technique
        hit every note perfect
        now
        you see?
        we have to invent things
        up here
        we call this *northern technology*"

RIVETT
        taking DENNIS HANSON's fiddle
        tunes it

        "sounds kinda raw
        . . . harsh!"

takes a blue comb
from his pocket

"i put this lil blue bird
here
        backka the bridge"

plays *the shannon waltz*
soft
        and sweet

and weeps
                till someone asks

                "DENNIS . . . did they
                play it
                at your wedding dance?"

"yes . . . yes
they did!"

RIVETT

    adjusting
    the fine-tuning screw
    . . . a tad
    for the last note

RIVETT

    an ambiguous smile
    chilling
    into a reflective gaze
    meeting my eyes

    "you know . . . up here
    when we talk of canada
    it's that place
            DOOOooun there!
            where the TERRITORIES end
            you know?
            we're still considered
            a colony here
            . . . remember that!"

1977 / 1979

HARRY DEBASTIEN IN THE MACKENZIE HOTEL PUB

1

hey . . . you know?
sometimes i go huntin
moose?
        come home with
        nothin?
        throw handful ah snow in
        pot?
        with tin tomato?
        got *moose track soup!*

hey . . . when INUVIK was first built?
was this MAGGIE one time
weighed 300 pounds
usttoo drink here at mackenzie
anyway . . . she was walkin home one night
an you know?
only two queen cowboy here that time
an this one?
he drivin down main street
an he kinda lonely?
see MAGGIE
he stop . . . say
"hey MAGGIE . . . come over here
i want to talk to you"

MAGGIE? she jus freeze
jus lay down on the walkway
this queen cowboy?
he try move her?
carry her to car?
he can't budge her
radio his friend
. . . an his friend
kinda lonely too
you know?
he come down
they try lift MAGGIE
no dice!
first queen cowboy say
"MAGGIE? MAGGIE go home"

3

hey . . . those days?
was this other MAGGIE
lived on snob hill
government an few others there
. . . poor people?
they lived in red square

anyway this MAGGIE?
taxi driver took her home from mackenzie
MAGGIE paid fare
slammed the door
taxi driver slowly drove home?
three blocks?
suddenly?
this knock on the window
he opened it . . . sez
"MAGGIE? i thought i jus drove you home"

MAGGIE sez
"yeh? but my parka!
got caught in the door!"

1977 / 1979

TO THE ONE

who woke
sunday morning
lying on a cold slab
of slate
when the INUVIK morgue
was still
a cabin

> *. . . wad um doin here?*
> *who dat fulla um fight*
> *in mackenzie*
> *los night . . .?*

and who rose to walk
dazedly
      down mackenzie avenue
      before the frozen
      observers

1979

DON AND LODDY

a square of bright
sunlight
illuminates
the posterpoem pinned
on the NORTH
                    wall
                    of the trailer

                    DON saying
                    "i came up here 7 years ago
                    finally had my fill
                    of that southern rat race
                    . . . had ulcers so bad
                    thought i'd die
                    anyway muh wife and i split up
                    for reasons of our own
                    the kids still write me sometimes
                    . . . yeah 6 months after i arrived
                    here in INUVIK
                    i was perfectly healed
                    no ulcers
                    and my head was clear
                    clear as that clean NORTHERN AIR
                    waftin in that trailer door

. . . no man
this is HOME now
ain't never goin down south again
never
. . . you oughta spend some time here
get to know these people
this PLACE
can't learn much in just a few days
only a few impressions
yeah man
you oughta live here awhile
you could throw your bottle of sanka
in the MACKENZIE
no need for that stuff here
. . . remember only one thing
when you come here

you don't come here with the intention
of teaching NORTHERNERS anything"

1977 / 1979

YOUNG INUIT ART STUDENT

FOR MISHA and MAKITUK

now slowly
remembering
cupping one hand
to scoop up water
        trickling it down
        MISHA's bronzed

                  hands

                    shaping

            the spinning

        ball of clay

the wordless communion
            me clumsily
            forming
gestures
            right hand
            a fist
                press
                down
left hand open
            push   a w a y !

a fist
      press
      down

MAKITUK watching
            MISHA a smile
            bright
            as summer's
            TUNRA SUN

. . . that day we three
became buddies!

the following day
MISHA
kneading clay
to hand-build
a perfect vessel

remembering

. . . using that naive
exuperyan touch
you drew a hand on it

and then
that i might be unafraid
of men who showed me fear
in a handful of dust
you drew an egyptian eye
in the palm
of that hand . . .

kootenay school of art
nelson, b.c. / 1967   *regina, sask. / 1979*

51

INUKSHUK

INUKSHUK

ESKIMO ROUTE

MARKER

STONE

IMAGE OF

AN INUIT HUNTER

STANDING SENTINEL

INUKSHUK

WHO SCARES

CARIBOU HERDS

TOWARDS

THE LIVING

HUNTERS

INUKSHUK

POINTING THE WAY

FOR MEN AND THE LONELY

CROSSING THE TUNDRA

1977 / 1979

CAMPBELL CREEK

sunday
      late afternoon
      the edge of CAMPBELL CREEK

      under warm NORTHERN SUN
      of late summer
      BILLY ascending the hill to the truck

      arriving
      BILLY pulling a huge northern pike
      from a white bag
      to shout at me

               "FISH!
               ONE FISH!"

      danny returning
      no fish

      me with two pike
      slightly smaller
      than BILLY's
      i swing them into BILLY's sack

               "your fish . . . BILLY
               three fish for you
               . . . for your mum
               brothers
               . . . an sisters"

               "foh me? good!
               THREE FISH!"

1977 / 1979

HUNTER STRANDED ON AN ICE FLOE

"When I was small, my father used to carry me on his back
when he went inland to hunt caribou. He went out hunting
one day, at the floe edge, with a younger boy, and my
mother, my little brother, and I were left alone. We were
out visiting, I think, when someone came to tell us that
they had found the sled and the dogs but there was no
sign of my father or his companion."
—PAINGUN KANAJUK from WE DON'T LIVE IN SNOW HOUSES NOW

1

in the kurelek painting
the ESKIMO hunter is seated on a triangular ice floe
his knees flexed
to contain the body warmth
and support folded arms on which to pillow
ancestral dreams
or the final dream of a dolphin
who returned as a whale
to carry him home

leant on something hidden behind the hunter
the harpoon rests
at an angle

kurelek explains
    "such a terrifying experience might happen
    when a hunter takes one
    too many chances
    pursuing a seal from floe to floe.
    to let himself fall
    into intensely cold water
    would mean certain death.
    there is nothing to be done
    but drift
    and wait."

2

hunter stranded on an ice floe
resembling so much
the ESKIMO sculpture i often admired
in the hudson's bay store that summer
back in the mountains
how i often fawned over it as an excuse to be there
till the beautiful sales woman
fell for me
as if i were a sea worth exploring

the sculpture
a triangular ice floe cut
from whale bone
a cross section revealing the marrow
small holes surrounding a larger one
aglu
'the breathing hole'
where the small ivory hunter with his harpoon
always knelt waiting
for a seal to rise
maybe a hunter like the very one kurelek painted
a hunter slowly drifting beyond the icy edge of home
unheeding the warnings of his father's ghost
that drifted the same way

that young woman drifted on like all the others
to the sea of what i hope
will be more merciful men
i have grown more wary of the heart the hunter
learning to settle for less
my one last dream
to return from where i am
as a whale
if there is anything left
to return to

1976 / 1979

EVENING CAMP

sunday
      evening camp
      CAMPBELL CREEK
in the cool shade
of tamaracks
         one
            by one

                JIMMY ALLARD turns
                BILLY's pike
                on two sticks

                "so simple man
                took an INDIAN
                to thinka this
                jus turn your fish
                over the campfire
                easy man . . .
                scales curling up
                bone dry
                . . . brush em away
                with a knife
                so simple!"

the children
cleaning BILLY's pike
JIMMY enjoying a cold beer
pulled from the creek

                somewhere beyond
                NORA's thin delicate fingers redden
                while she picks cranberries
                sweetened
                by the first frost

and far beyond her
on the edge
of precambrian stone
others are harvesting the last
blue
        and yellow berries

far beyond them
and NORA
"the meaning of NORTH"
the stooped ambling GHOST
of GREAT GRANDFATHER
MASUZUMI
who emigrated from japan
is checking the abandoned
traps
        rusting along
        the northern edge
of the BERING STRAIT

ANGATKROK
                and other whales

circling

                in the deep green
of the
                BEAUFORT SEA

while little NOAH
age 3
brushes another
                sandfly
from his forehead

1977 / 1979

RUTH CARROLL SPEAKS OF NEHTROO

"NEHTROO
he take the skin
from a caribou's legs?
and he put strips of it
under runners
of a lil sleigh?
then he put some driftwood
inside it
an he's pullin the sleigh
real fast?
. . . now i
can't quite remember
i think he stop
maybe rest?
there someone jump on wood inside
and you know?
it make these cracking sounds?
anyway . . . my mother
use to say
'that driftwood it broke
like falling dishes'
. . . it was a good story
when i was a lil girl
but later it confuse me
cause long ago
they never had no dishes up here?
where did they come from?
i don't know
maybe the lil kids
they had some kind lil
toy dishes
. . . anyway
that's my favorite story
about NEHTROO
i forgot the rest"

1977 / 1979

THE ARENA

1

friday night dance at the arena
on the edge of INUVIK
labatt's blue night pervading
my thoughts

impinging images of the appropriators
using the land
using the people
and using the woman

news travelling
like a candling
bush fire

"... hey
you know that television crew
that arrived yesterday?
well the camera man
put the make on MISHA's wife
MISHA jumped outta his cab
came in ... was gonna
pummel the caribou shit outta him
... found out the guy was
here with the others
doin a thing on the pipeline
so he said
                "fine man ... let you go this time
                next time ... i'll scatter you
                piece by piece
                over THE DELTA!"

2

MABEL
tired of it all
bushed with the whole mindboggling charade
bushed with the stories

       . . . men who whisper sweet offerings
       of whiskey
       and a free room

MABEL
worn by the pain

       labatt's blue won't soften
       the pain of loss
       . . . saying goodbye
       to her two native children
       leaving with the southern white father
       who boarded the pacific western flight south
       this morning

MABEL
so tired

      of all this caribou crap
     turns on me
     wearing my new cap
     with the TERRITORIAL LOGO:

          WHITE
          POLAR
          BEAR

     set against

          DEEP BLUE

"YOU WEAR THAT FUCKING CAP!
BUT YOU DON'T WEAR IT
. . . WITH DIGNITY!"

1977 / 1979

LETTER TO EDDIE BAZIE

"And the same stars
To look after us
The same hearts
And the same minds
To love us
And to carry us
When we need help
To keep on goin'
On and on
The strength of the old
To remind us
The smiles of the children
To keep us keeping on
For those who brought us this far"

EDDIE BAZIE

dear EDDIE:
            . . . from your new year's resolution
For the Old People they are my favorite words today
the bright MACKENZIE flows quietly to the sea
i'm on a plane
about to leave for NORMAN WELLS
                                    three years
i've communed with your GHOST still looming
over the northern parkland beyond the pen
and trying to find its way back home to RAE
your GHOST
            EDDIE
                    has always honored your memory
and refuses to tell me anything about you
and why should it?

                   earlier in the week EDDIE
down in YELLOWKNIFE
i met ALPHONSE SIMPSON from RAE
we drank in the rec hall
where he told me how fine a drum you played
for that band
you guys got together in RAE
                              i also met
WILLIAM BALSILLIE who said he also knew you
said his brother was one of your best friends
said "yeah . . . sure man . . . i danced to his music
whenever they came down to YELLOWKNIFE"
                                        i met a guy
down south once
an OJIBWAY called CHRIS
who said he knew of you in the pen
if you had trouble sleeping at times there
and heard those drumsticks
working out new rhythms on a small rubber pad
 in cell somewhere
                    that was CHRIS
                    beating it out 14 hours a day
                    the stations of the cross
                    as a drum solo

you know EDDIE
one night in a friend's METIS shack
in ST. BONIFACE
i heard that young CHRIS
do a four hour drum solo
at times it was chilling
seemed like someone else took over
the sticks
to give him a breather
was it you . . . EDDIE?

there's something haunting
about the beauty of people in the NORTH here
something about those faces
especially the young
sometimes an oriental beauty
                              EDDIE the plane
is moving out to the runway
and i don't know what it is
the airport sign reading
                    INUVIK
                    ELEV 223
                              is beginning to blur
i know i've not been here long enough
to really know your place
your people
or why you had to leave RAE
to go south to die
in the prison
of a foreign country

          i don't know EDDIE
          i don't know

Note: EDDIE BAZIE hanged himself in the Prince Albert Penitentiary the day after Christmas, 1972. He was 23.

1974 / 1977 / 1979

Andrew Suknaski, the Wood Mountain poet, has published over twenty chapbooks and major collections of poetry over the past ten years. Among his major collections are WOOD MOUNTAIN POEMS (Macmillan, 1976) and THE GHOSTS CALL YOU POOR (Macmillan, 1978). The latter book was awarded the Canadian Authors Association Prize as the best Canadian poetry book of 1978. Suknaski and his poetry is the subject material of a recent NFB film called WOOD MOUNTAIN POEMS.

EAST OF MYLOONA also reveals Suknaski's artistic talents. He has studied art at the Kootenay School of Art and in Montreal. His poem/drawings have appeared in international exhibitions, and his woodcut prints have been featured in a number of his books. The drawings in EAST OF MYLOONA were completed at the University of Manitoba during the winter of 1977/78 when Suknaski was Writer-in-Residence there.

THISTLEDOWN BOOKS

WIND SONGS by Glen Sorestad

DARK HONEY by Ronald Marken

INSIDE IS THE SKY by Lorna Uher

OCTOMI by Andrew Suknaski

SUMMER'S BRIGHT BLOOD by William Latta

PRAIRIE PUB POEMS by Glen Sorestad

PORTRAITS by Lala Koehn

HAIL STORM by Peter Christensen

BETWEEN THE LINES by Stephen Scriver

GATHERING FIRE by Helen Hawley

TOWARDS A NEW COMPASS by Lorne Daniel

NOW IS A FAR COUNTRY by John V. Hicks

OLD WIVES LAKE by J. D. Fry

THE CURRIED CHICKEN APOCALYPSE by Michael Cullen

ANCESTRAL DANCES by Glen Sorestad

EAST OF MYLOONA by Andrew Suknaski

DATE DUE